The One-Minute Healing Experience

Now there are no excuses
for not having enough time.
Ellen Laura has devised a method
that only takes a minute.
In sixty seconds you can heal a hurt feeling,
a loss, a frustration, or a fear.
Read this healing book and regain the brilliance
and clarity you desire in your life.
Then take a minute to tell a friend.

—Janice Wilson, M.A., author,
The Gift from the Goddess

What people are saying about
The One-Minute Healing Experience by Ellen Laura

"*The One-Minute Healing Experience* is but an instant away. Ellen Laura directs the reader into the balance of faith and wellness. Her book is compelling, spirit-filled, and loving. I have given this book to several of my friends and the effect is explosive. . . . Everyone asks for a copy to pass on to someone special. This book is a heart-warming must."

Sandee Boots Tiberti, national director, St. Jude's Ranch

"After reading *The One-Minute Healing Experience*, I rediscovered my ability to recognize healing moments as they happened—they come so frequently! I now know how to attract the information I need to help me unfold, or receive vital answers to questions I have asked of the universe. Healing moments can come from anywhere, as I learned from this marvelous book, even from animals. All we need is the encouragement and support to *BE still, listen, and be patient.*"

Kim Driggs, Avatar Marketing

"As a teacher of meditation for thirty years, my life has been devoted to spiritual unfoldment and transcendence. Since my journey to India in 1969, I often search for the simplicity of explanation that comes out so beautifully in this little gem of a book. Ellen Laura insists that time is not a major factor affecting our unfoldment, and I wholeheartedly agree."

Beverlee Cannon, director, Ayurvedic Living Center

"*The One-Minute Healing Experience* is warm, inspirational, affirmational—in a word, wonderful. It is a practical treatise on how to become aware of the daily miracles in life. Read it and you will see all things, people, ideas in a new Light.

John Scevola, author, Sales Dragon™

Move beyond time to experience
your own awakening and healing.

The
One-Minute
Healing Experience

◆

Ellen M. Laura

Blue Dolphin Publishing
1997

Published by Blue Dolphin Publishing, Inc.
P.O. Box 8, Nevada City, CA 95959
Orders: 1-800-643-0765

ISBN: 1-57733-012-9

Library of Congress Cataloging-in-Publication Data

Laura, Ellen M., 1949–
    The one-minute healing experience / Ellen M. Laura.
      p.   cm.
    ISBN 1-57733-012-9
    1. Spiritual healing.   2. Laura, Ellen M., 1949–   . I. Title.
BL65.M4L38 1997
158—dc21   97-14227
                                         CIP

Cover by: Dawn Lynn & Carolyn Hamilton-Proctor

Printed in Canada

10   9   8   7   6   5   4   3   2   1

Dedicated with love
to
Tom Matejko

Contents

Acknowledgments

My love and appreciation to: Dawn Lynn, my spiritual friend who encouraged me to continue working when it would have been easier to abandon this project; to Alokiam and Huenda, for celebrating and sharing their eternal love with each of us; to Saundra Corinth, for inspiring me with the essence of her crystal clear heart; to MJ Valente, for her unwavering loyalty and support; to Nancy Gott, M.A., for her insightful gentleness and editorial assistance; and to the Golden Plovers, for caring about each of us.

Introduction

by Robert D. Milne, M.D.

Over the past decades, interest and concern has increased about the nature of our health system. Estimates indicate the leading causes of death in our society—heart disease, high blood pressure, cancer, and accidents—are all directly linked to the way we live. Diseases of lifestyle are predicted to be an increasing menace as we enter the next century. We are once again reminded of the necessity for personal responsibility in all areas of life. *In order to achieve optimal health, a state of harmony between our physical, mental, and spiritual energy systems must be created.*

Fortunately, some of the barriers between conventional Western medicine and complementary (holistic) medicine are beginning to break down. My own interest in complementary medicine started when my daughter Brooke became very ill and was unable to be helped by drug medicines. After many months of illness, in desperation, I was introduced to homeopathy. My daughter's health returned rapidly. Since then I have traveled to Europe in search of methods to help my patients. I have discovered a vast network of people who want and deserve answers about health and healing on all levels.

The patients I see come from all over the world. I strive to impart an essential point to each person: *The body, mind, and spirit of a human being are inseparable, and one cannot be affected without comparably affecting the other two.* Understanding this concept is the principle that makes self-regulation and healing possible.

Many studies demonstrate that spiritual well-being can often affect our mental and bodily functions. New research reveals that people who develop spiritual stamina recover from stress and illnesses more quickly. Spiritual enlightenment is a very personal, individualized process.

Few doctors have time to give in-depth counseling about the connection between body, mind, and soul. The search for physical and spiritual well-being is not an easy one. This is a book that any doctor could enthusiastically recommend to their patients, friends, and families, because it is universal and focuses on preventive medicine for the Soul.

While reading this book, a marvelous feeling of participation inevitably emerges. This material will empower anyone who has experienced feelings of despair, longing, or unfulfilled dreams, while looking for spiritual meaning. Ellen creates an instant rapport with the reader, regardless of age or sex. As soon as I finished reading the book, I recommended that my wife and children read it, because Ellen's humanistic warmth, care, and respect for the individual reader are apparent. Many inspirational books are so lofty, the reader may feel isolated. This book offers the much-needed and often ignored inclusion. It is an outstanding book, and deserves to be read and reread by anyone who wants to achieve excellent health of body, mind, and spirit.

Awaken to Miracles
of the Moment

Instances of spontaneous, miraculous healing have baffled doctors and scientists for centuries. They recognize that a healing has occurred, but have no explanation. Others believe that all things are possible, because they know that God's holy power is on duty every minute of every day, like a benevolent friend, awaiting our awakening. This awesome power, which resides within each of us, offers us the possibility of instant healing and relief from daily stress, confusion, pain, or illness—and is always readily available. Too often we seek help from others who are misguided, running here and there after this teacher or that healer. Ultimately, every genuine teacher insists that we go within and honor our own inner power.

1

This book offers companionship as it encourages you to open the door to your silent heart chamber, where a special healing moment may be waiting to take place for you. In one, timeless flash, a problem or illness which has drained you could dissolve. *IT IS possible to have healing experiences that are not governed by time . . . and you can awaken to miracles of the moment.*

Over the past twenty-five years I have met many people who have experienced instantaneous healing and the realms of pure light and sound where these moments originate. Each special meeting causes me to recall the insightful words from Richard Bach's book, *Illusions:* "Your friends will know you better in the first minute you meet, than your acquaintances will know you in a thousand years."

Throughout history there have been references to people who have made sacred journeys to remote areas and reported instantaneous healing—*experiences that do not fit into the linear time frame we have constructed.* In my search for spiritual wisdom I continue to find validation for nontraditional healing, both in current writing and from masters of other eras. Plato, Pythagoras, Rumi, Lao Tzu, Buddha, and Jesus have reached beyond the boundaries of time, encouraging us to expect miracles because they are our birthright. This book is about people becoming transformed by instantaneous healing.

My sacred journey has not involved travel to exotic places. My life began in a "little Italian / Catholic town" in central New York, where most people reject change and cling to long-established habits, regardless of whether they bring joy or misery.

My first experience related to this subject occurred almost thirty years ago. In November 1968, I told my family I planned to marry my high school sweetheart—in two weeks! My father expressed outrage about my impetuous decision, insisting he would not attend. Why would I marry a "boy" about to be shipped overseas to Vietnam? Was I pregnant, he demanded to know. Defying my father's wishes, I married for the first time on November 6, 1968.

A month later, while combing my hair and admiring my grown-up, nineteen-year-old reflection in the bedroom mirror, my mother knocked loudly at the door, interrupting my daydreams. Standing there with my mother was a Marine officer in full dress uniform. The panic on my mother's face and the officer's military uniform rang out like a shot piercing my heart. The Lieutenant removed a telegram from his pocket.

He began to read: *"I deeply regret to confirm that your husband died on December 19, 1968. He sustained gunshot wounds to the body from hostile rifle fire while on patrol. His mother has been notified."*

Without warning, my love—a child's fragrant bed of roses—became a bed of thorns. I grabbed the dreaded paper from his hands, called him a murderer, and told him to get out. The hours and days that followed are muffled in my memory. Mixed with the nightmare images of my young husband's tragic death were fragments of a dream I recalled from the night of the fatal shooting. Each day, new images from that full-color dream crept closer to my conscious mind.

This was long before people openly communicated about "near death experiences," so I lacked a reference point for this "other reality." In this vivid, animated dream, I felt myself being "taken home." A voice that seemed to be both inside me and coming from "home," spoke out: *From the wing of an eagle, the top of the mountain I have glimpsed.*

The voice grew louder and repeated, *"From the wing of an eagle, the top of the mountain I have glimpsed."* Suddenly, I was on top of the mountain. From the mountain peak the world was a brilliant, shimmering white and gold; there a waterfall beckoned to me. The water appeared to be made of an electric, sparkling substance that changed from powdery white to purely translucent. As I moved deeper into this pulsing sea of energy, I heard the single note of a flute, and it moved me to the core of my being. The sound continued until my being vibrated and became an instrument for the heavenly music. The inner voice continued, *"Yes, you have entered the spiritual heavens, but not through any power of your own. One who loves you deeply has granted you this glimpse of heaven. You can never turn back once you set your feet on this royal highway."* I awoke drenched with a sweet silence that opened the door to an ecstatic love—this was home.

During the funeral and the weeks following, my behavior grew stranger than ever. One minute I would burst out laughing, then find myself flooded with grief. *I found it impossible to explain that I missed that place called home more than I missed my young husband.* My parents felt embarrassed and frightened. I refused to go to the cemetery, insisting that Brian was not in the ground; I knew he was in heaven.

At the time of that experience, I considered religion to be silly and unnecessary. I never prayed. I wasn't a kind or nurturing person, and I didn't change overnight. Actually, it was years before any qualities that are typically considered spiritual became noticeable. Instead, I was left with a burning passion to know and understand the *source* of that experience.

I began reading volumes of spiritual poetry, philosophy, and autobiographies of saints and mystics. I investigated dozens of spiritual groups, each claiming to have the highest and most direct path to God. I continued on my quest to return "home," often feeling like an abandoned ET. I was drawn to the saints who were intoxicated with love for God; their teachings guided me to my own place of power and healing.

During those years I learned valuable spiritual practices that allowed me to experience higher states of consciousness, and I continue those practices now. The clear, translucent light and the familiar spiritual presence continued to quietly guide my life and bring blessings, although there were long periods when I did not discuss them with anyone.

The next experience that relates significantly to why this book is in your hands occurred in 1980, while I was living in Los Angeles. That was the year I met my present husband. I heard about a healing center in Baja, Mexico, and felt drawn there. I drove to the Plaza Santa Maria hospital and applied for a job. Medical doctors, chiropractors, massage therapists, and psychologists were there. They gathered to practice alternative healing methods, primarily for cancer patients (this was the clinic that received so much publicity when actor Steve McQueen sought treatment there).

I was hired as assistant to the financial controller of the hospital, Tom Matejko. Tom was a fireball, working sixteen to eighteen hours each day, and his passion for the hospital's work affected every patient and doctor. Tom and an associate went to Mexico to offer alternative healing unavailable in the United States. The men and women who worked together in the hospital did not want anyone to be denied a place to heal.

I learned that Tom's twenty-nine-year-old wife, Patricia, died of cancer only four months before. The staff psychologist was constantly hounding Tom; he feared that he was in denial and avoiding his grief. I gently questioned him, and he revealed his experience, one that paralleled my own. After Patricia passed on, several spiritual beings took him to a wondrous world of white and gold. Tom heard the single note of a flute, and his anguish dissolved. Of course, he had experienced moments of deep sadness, but he also possessed a knowing that only her physical body passed on. He was sparkling with energy and his eyes danced when he recalled this experience.

Tom avoided thinking about his spiritual experience since Patricia's funeral. When he had spoken about heaven then, as if he knew it, his relatives thought he was hallucinating. After Tom finished relating his story, I remembered making an affirmation, *"I want a man who loves God as much as I do."* I then knew what had drawn me to Mexico.

A few months ago, I was reminded about why we are together, and this book was conceived that day.

Tom was rushing off to work and I was preparing to teach a yoga class when my friend Saundra arrived. Tom rarely opens his heart to my female friends, but he connected with Saundra in a special way from their first meeting and often looked to her for spiritual guidance and encouragement. On this morning, she whisked by Tom, giving him a brief hello, and continued directly to class.

Later, Saundra confided her intuition that Tom might have felt slighted by her brief greeting. Upon his return home that evening, I told Tom that Saundra sent her love to him. "Really?" he responded. "This morning she didn't even have time to give me a *One-Minute Healing!*"

When he spoke those words, chills swept through my body. Suddenly, a flash of light filled the room, the atmosphere changed, and I heard the unmistakable inner voice say, *"When Saundra or any sincere person sends pure love or light to Tom, he is awakened to a 'One-Minute Healing.' Now you can tell everyone what Tom already knows—miracles don't run by a clock."*

Energy Flows
Where Attention Goes

For five decades, research has shown how excessive stress accelerates the aging process and creates havoc in our brains. When a mouse is placed on an electric grid and given mild shocks, its body begins to break down after each shock, and the mouse dies in just a few days.

Autopsies reveal signs of accelerated aging, but because the shocks were mild, the cause of death is not the shocks, but the mouse's reaction to the stress: its own body killed itself! It is the continuous stress (shocks) and the stress hormones that are released in response to the stress that kill the mouse. When the mouse has time to recover between shocks, little to no harm occurs. *When overloaded with stress, the small miracles in life go unnoticed and unappreciated. Think about the implications for humans and how we could benefit if we would take time to recover from stress by using methods that guide us to the temple within.*

Many people mistakenly believe that the time factor involved in recovering from stress and disappointment is beyond their reach. "If only I had time, I'd take care of myself," is a common complaint. Why we have agreed on this distorted viewpoint, making time our "holy savior," is a mystery to me. Research now shows that it is not more leisure time we need to overcome modern stress—it is a healthy lifestyle that has greater meaning. *What we really need more time for is to count and multiply our blessings.* Our confusion about time increases our frustration about internal and external stress-producing events. *When you learn to decrease your internal stress, your mind and heart will participate, not rebel, in finding ways to decrease external stress.*

External stress comes from outside events—such as financial, environmental, and social pressures. Stressful conditions, such as air pollution, toxic waste accidents, or being $30,000 in credit card debt, typically require time to rectify. Of equal or even greater concern are the invisible, internal stressors. They include the condition of our body and brain chemistry, attitudes, emotions, and thoughts. Whether the stress is internal or external (often they intermingle), *the way you respond determines whether your body releases harmful stress hormones or not.*

For instance, if your teenager is loudly playing his stereo, it can cause external and internal stress (unless you are wearing earplugs). The external stress comes from the harsh, nerve-wracking noise, while the internal stress comes from your turbulent thoughts and emotions about his behavior and the music. Internal and external pressures abound in our callous and metallic society, making us look frazzled and haggard, and draining our natural ability to be joyful and creative—regardless of our biological age.

Several years ago, while I was in the midst of teaching a stress-reducing exercise class, one of my students commented that she lived a stress-free life. I knew her external stress was minimal, and there were no financial pressures in her life. Yet, she wore the sullen, tight-lipped look of a frustrated woman and appeared much older than her biological age. She wasn't suffering from any physical illness; it was internal stress that depleted her energy. Like many people, she insisted she was happy, but her face revealed the truth—invisible stress marched across her forehead and around her mouth, leaving unmistakable marks of discouragement and defeat.

The list of worries causing internal stress and disrupting inner relaxation is endless: Is your mate cheating on you? Will your children be harmed at the next basketball game they attend? Is your business partner scheming to get rid of you? Will that dreaded illness strike again? Will your climb up the corporate ladder provide financial security, or leave you empty and unfulfilled? When the large issues are not nagging us, the smaller ones provide an incessant poking and pinching that is just as insidious. Shall I call and get a price quote on repairing my roof, or hope it doesn't rain again; shall I take my dog to the vet tonight, or wait until morning; shall I tell my wife that her bad breath turns me off?

Poison seeps into our lives from these tedious thoughts and drains us more than we'd like to admit. Few people know how to recover from these thoughts and feelings. Don't wait until you are suffocating in the quicksand of physical or psychological pain before you consider *preventive spiritual medicine*. Invisible stress can do more than ruin your looks and your love life; it can cause you to forget why you are on Earth, and drain the life force and power you need to propel yourself into a meaningful future.

My most significant discovery is this: *The spiritual presence always desires to make itself known to us and bestow blessings. The sharp talons of time and internal stress distract us and keep us from making a daily visit to the temple within. When things are not going well in our lives, we must review our contracts and agreements with time and stress. Every second is precious and has already been committed to God, whether we recall the commitment or not.*

Energy Flows Where Attention Goes

Our addiction to stress attracts negative currents of energy that greedily destroy our passion for life. Unfortunately, we have become so accustomed (or numbed) to these negative energies invading us that we believe this is the only way to survive. Until the addiction to negative energies is recognized and effectively dealt with, we will remain mystified about balancing our spiritual and physical (sensuous) energy.

Energy from the pure spiritual realms enters through the crown of the head, linking us with the source of creativity and compassion. Energy also flows upward from the Earth into our bodies, to make us passionate and powerful. These mingling energies can create chaos and crime, or ecstasy and enthusiasm.

We are responsible for balancing these energies. Repressed emotions and destructive thought patterns create an inner volcano that interferes with our ability to balance these energies and recover from stress. The ageless wisdom taught by saints and sages can guide us gently toward balance and teach us to recognize and honor our individual differences.

Knowing how to make the right lifestyle choices for our individuality is of great importance in this balancing act. Wisdom comes from sources that appear to have little to do with spirituality, yet on deeper reflection, life's lessons are everywhere. An important message came from the Chinese team coach, after winning the 1984 Olympics, gold medal in ping-pong: *"Here is our philosophy: If you develop your strengths to the maximum, the strength becomes so great it overwhelms the weaknesses. Our winning player, you see, plays only his forehand. Even though he cannot play backhand and his competition knows he cannot play backhand, his forehand is so invincible that it cannot be beaten."*

When you focus on reinforcing your strengths instead of fretting about your weaknesses, you will find you are more lovable and attractive than you ever imagined—especially to yourself and to those who appreciate your uniqueness. If you feel stuck, look at the people you spend time with. Nothing slows down spiritual awakening more than inappropriate associations.

If you forget everything else, remember this: Your energy is intended to be a glorious intermingling of creativity, compassion, power, and passion—shared and appreciated by others. As you come to realize this for yourself, you can awaken to healing moments, keep them cycling through your life, and reverse the downward pull of negativity.

Since miracles don't run by a clock, time is not the major issue here. The issue is energy and rejuvenation— most people lack the balanced, harmonious energy flow needed to "turn on" the inner light and sound, magnetize moments of healing, and rebound from disappointment and illness. Employing powerful spiritual practices on a daily basis reveals the meaning that seems to be missing from our lives.

In the book by Brian Walker, *Hua Hu Ching, The Unknown Teaching of Lao Tzu,* it states:

The universe is a vast net of energy rays. The primary ray is that which emanates from the Subtle Origin, and it is entirely positive, creative, and constructive. Each being, however, converts the energy of this primary ray into its own ray, and these lower rays can be either positive or negative, constructive or destructive. To attain full evolution and the status of an integral being, you must be aware of this intricate net and its influences upon you. By integrating the positive, harmonious rays with the positive elements of your own being, and eliminating the subtle negative influences, you can enhance all aspects of your life.

This good and gentle energy shows us how to attain greatness and regain our lost nobility. The inner power must be summoned and welcomed as our beloved. *If it doesn't come as quickly or stay as long as we wish, we must look within, feel, and listen. Ask: Have I created a sanctuary for the inner power, or a doghouse where an occasional old bone is tossed out to quiet the howling? What thoughts and feelings fill the spaces within my heart and mind? What power would find a home inside of me?*

Many people see themselves as insignificant and small, so the only power they invite is one that desires authority and dominance over them. Others have gone to the opposite extreme, by falsely inflating themselves. If our individual consciousness is crowded with thoughts of imperfection and separateness, where is there room for that good and gentle power to live? To build an inner sanctuary, we must fill ourselves with more stars, more fragrance, more love, and more light. We must continue constructing the sanctuary until the Divine takes up residence in our hearts and the sound current sweeps us toward the heavens. On a practical level, start looking and listening to the people you consider friends, and ask yourself: Who and what have I let in through the front door?

It Takes Only One Minute to Choose

Obviously, it takes more than one minute to accomplish a purpose with the magnitude of Mother Teresa or Mahatma Gandhi, to write a great novel, or to do a good job raising a child. However, all of these accomplishments flow from choices made moment by moment.

During difficult moments, grace may guide us to a person or place to lead us out of our difficulties and release us from the chains that bind us to our self-created prisons. When life's rough and rocky bumps knock us down, we quickly forget most of the inspirational stories and "growth techniques" we've read or heard. *But, we don't have to forget! All the truth and wisdom around us can become a part of our moment-to-moment consciousness, when we awaken to it.*

Preventive Medicine for the Soul

A parade of products proclaim their ability to make you healthy, wealthy, and wise. *All of this would be wonderful if it really motivated you to breathe in the bliss flowing from the atmosphere of Divine Source, reinforce your strengths, and discover your soul path.* Yet, with all of these "tools of enlightenment" available, how many smiling faces and happy hearts do you meet every day? Indulging in the expanding stream of "magical" healing products, seminars, and services is often a distraction that feeds the debt cycle. It would be wise to consider that "less is better" when approaching spiritual unfoldment.

Consider this: It is possible to rebound from the stress you meet each day, and to live long enough to fulfill your purpose and destiny—whether twenty years or one-hundred-and-twenty years! You can build spiritual stamina and experience triumph at the completion of each life cycle. *A journey to the temple within on a daily basis is the most important step in awakening your Higher Self.* You can do this by rearranging your life to make room for eternal and constant blessings. You can awaken to miracles of the moment.

Recognizing
a One-Minute
Healing Experience

A *One-Minute Healing Experience* is significantly more beneficial and brings more blessings than a dry, mental concept or a warm, fuzzy feeling. This experience involves a tangible shift in consciousness that transforms feelings and thoughts, and occasionally involves pleasant sensations in the body. Some people experience a quick rush or chill that brings a subtle smile, deep peace, or cleansing tears. Others feel the atmosphere around them become light, blissful, spacious, or charged with strength and courage.

This change in personal atmosphere is highly significant, because it marks the experience as much more than an intellectual insight or an "aha." If we look up toward the sky and see enormous, dark clouds blocking the sun, it is obvious that some force or energy must empty or move the clouds before sunshine can fill the sky. *A change in atmosphere precedes outer change.*

Attempting to change behavior without some shift in the inner atmosphere leads to frustration. Our inner atmosphere is permeated by an intricate pattern of beliefs, feelings, and thoughts about our worth and value and our relationship to the Divine Source. Our inner being is able to impregnate the atmosphere with bliss, wisdom, courage, and other spiritual qualities. This can occur as an act of grace, through devotion to spiritual practices, or a combination of both.

Often people comment that they find it easier to relax or meditate when they are in a certain spiritual environment. This is because each place has an atmosphere, whether we have trained ourselves to be aware of it or not.

A story about Lord Buddha illustrates the power of atmosphere. Lord Buddha performed many spiritual disciplines, and one of these consisted of maintaining silence, inner and outer. Many learned teachers and scholars wanted to disturb his silence and hold debates with him. But the atmosphere about

Buddha was so charged with his *silence* that the moment those scholars entered his atmosphere, they forgot all about their plan to have a debate with him, and they became silent. They would sit silently in the presence of Buddha and came back uplifted. Such is the effect of atmosphere.

Every *"One-Minute Healing Experience"* I know of has produced a significant shift, inside the person first, and then outer conditions change as a result. An example of this shift in atmosphere occurred in 1989, when my beloved fourteen-year-old Persian cat, Shamus, died unexpectedly. Through my grieving, a nagging thought plagued my mind, creating internal stress: Shamus had outlasted any husband or job to date—we shared fourteen years of commitment, and that was a record for me! That fluffy, feisty cat was my traveling companion and confidante from Las Vegas to Los Angeles, New York, Wisconsin, Oregon, and back to New York! The more I chewed on this thought, the more impossible it became to relax. *Yes, I knew that death was not the end of life, but when the mind starts chewing, the transformative power of wisdom vanishes.*

After hours of crying and a feeling of intense pressure in my chest, I decided to call a few close friends. The first friend was kind and patient and attempted to console me by saying it was normal to feel terrible after such a loss. When we hung up, I relaxed a bit (the clouds shifted slightly, but they were still hanging heavy). My next call was to one of my most important spiritual allies and a dear friend, Jerry Wolcott.

I sobbed out my distress. He listened for one or two minutes and asked me a few questions. As I listened to his voice, I suddenly felt a shift in my personal atmosphere, and the pain in my chest dissolved. My voice changed, my emotions settled, I relaxed deeply, and I found myself smiling. "Shamus is all right," I said. *"Yes, he is, and so are you,"* Jerry responded. I instantly recognized this moment for the genuine blessing it held for me.

That experience was similar in quality to the one I experienced when my first husband died, where my sadness disappeared and dissolved into the light. *These powerful experiences are intended to guide our lives.* Although they often involve healing and releasing of pain, they also come to help us connect with our true friends and lovers. For anyone who cannot recall such an experience, remember: *acknowledging small blessings and miracles creates the atmosphere that attracts the dramatic ones.*

**One-minute healing experiences
awaken us in many ways:**

◆ You recognize that a draining pain or burden has left you, and it doesn't return.

◆ You feel a great generosity of spirit.

◆ You find yourself not "trying so hard."

◆ You are more aware of your personal boundaries and you won't allow people to waste your time or steal your energy.

◆ You stop making promises you can't keep, to yourself and others.

◆ Your desire to manipulate, control, and change others diminishes and eventually fades away.

◆ You say good-bye to the "victim/martyr-drama" syndrome.

◆ You stop tolerating and start living.

◆ You are kinder to yourself and others— self-criticism and prejudice dissolve.

◆ You know how to balance a "soft heart" with a "sharp head."

◆ You develop a finely-tuned awareness to all shifts in atmosphere.

◆

If you've ever been lost in a nightmare,
it may have been a One-Minute Healer
who reached out to help you,
but they would never follow you into darkness.

◆

How to Use
This Book

Four sections follow:

Love & Kindness

Longevity & Rejuvenation

Prosperity & Abundance

Wisdom & Responsibility

The stories that follow are about people facing real life challenges and reaping substantial spiritual rewards. What these people have discovered is this: It isn't necessary to mentally understand every detail of our consciousness to attract healing moments, any more than it is necessary to understand the detailed workings of electricity to turn on the lights.

It's the "turning on" and balancing process that's important. Spiritual energy from the Divine Source ignites the heart and soul. Once this energy is turned on, it must remain activated moment-to-moment; otherwise we operate like mechanical robots. *We know our spiritual energy is activated when we are able to change the flow of our thoughts and emotions from a downward, polluted, life-draining spiral to a clean, upward, energy-expanding spiral.*

When we forget the importance of being still and serene, we find our ability to change the flow is disrupted, and we deprive ourselves from experiencing the greatest joy God has extended to us. This does not imply that we are "bad" or negative, simply that our attention lacks a spiritual focus. Never be deceived—anyone who is unable to be still is hiding from the Higher Self.

Being centered in stillness opens the door to the temple within. Only at this stage of awareness do we begin to glimpse the gift of flowing with the stream of imagination. *Our ability to manifest miracles depends on our relationship to silence and continuous imagination. This is the key to happiness that we have longed for in our most private moments.*

If you have been studying healing and spiritual-growth practices for years and you still don't know how to shift your focus to God in an instant, re-evaluate your dedication and sincerity, or look for a new teacher. If these practices are new to you, wonderful; you are starting with an openness and curiosity that invites success.

Each story you are about to read holds a deeply personal message for you and involves some aspect of healing and enrichment. At first glance this may not be apparent. You may say, "My circumstances are entirely different; this doesn't relate to me." When you have a strong reaction to a story, either positive or negative, pay close attention. These are typically the areas of consciousness that are rigid and interfere with being "turned-on."

All that is necessary to unlock the message of each story is this: *Take several deep breaths, relax, and enter your personal sanctuary.* If you have knots or tightness in your chest or stomach, relax and release. Pause for a moment, close your eyes, and affirm with feeling: "I inhale the breath of divine purity and bliss, and effortlessly release all fatigue and tightness." Many people say they lack the ability to visualize, but most of us possess the ability to *FEEL,* and *HARMONIOUS FEELING* is a key ingredient in creating a new state of consciousness. Move gracefully—don't rush—continue to welcome the light and sound of God as you read. It doesn't matter if you are a skeptic or a strong believer. You will receive blessings.

If you want help, consider calling on those spiritual beings who guided me to write this book. They often leave their signature as a golden crescent when they appear, and I have come to know them as Golden Plovers. Many people have seen or experienced their protection and love and know them by different names, such as the Magi or Wise Men who appeared before Christ was born.

The stories range from subtle to dramatic and involve seemingly ordinary people. Appearances are rarely what they seem to be, so ask yourself: who is ordinary? *My discovery has been this: We are all spiritual beings with infinite worth and value—not one of us is ordinary!*

Love & Kindness

Some people wake up, look at a sunrise, or into the eyes of their loved ones, and smile because they know God loves them. Others wake up frightened, lonely, and heartbroken. Most of us live somewhere in between. It is this in between realm where love and kindness seek rebirth.

◆

Love is a living substance
and can be pure and strong, or
diluted with many other feelings and intentions.
Those who care can open their hearts
and receive this flow of love
directly from its Source.

◆

To thrive and prosper, it is necessary to have love and good thoughts from each person who is close to us. *It is through this daily flow of love that our inner powers expand and a channel of love opens between ourselves, the world, and Spirit.* It is dangerous and draining to surround ourselves with people who harbor feelings of resentment and ill-will toward us. If you live or work with people who resent, fear, or envy you, don't be surprised if it takes longer for you to recover from illness or injury. Every endeavor, every project takes twice as long as it should because of the energy drain of resentment! Love is not a luxury, it is a necessity.

Many people talk about love, but too often it is a lifeless, dead image they speak of. Talking about water does not quench your thirst, and talking about love does not attract miracles. Once your inner light is activated, you can appreciate and attract love.

If you are ready to hitch a ride on the "Love Shuttle" as it continues to move between Heaven and Earth and back again, fill yourself with love and kindness. You already possess the ticket; just go to the temple within to claim it!

Clean, Golden Threads of Love

When people experience love, a golden thread, made of cords of light, connects them heart to heart. This can be between lovers, friends, or between parents and children. Few people know about this, because the thread is invisible, so they fail to cherish and take care of it. When the thread is clean, it sparkles, and feelings of joy, tenderness, happiness, ecstasy, kindness, and bliss flow from one person to another.

◆

Megan's mother was kind and gentle, and as a child Megan loved her deeply. Her mother spent her days cooking, making her house sparkle and shine, and taking care of her family. Megan could always remember how sweet her mother smelled and how comforting her touch felt. In her innocence, Megan felt nourished by her mother's love, not realizing she lived with a rare treasure.

As a teenager Megan began to notice her mother lacked the style and savvy she saw in magazines and on TV, and this embarrassed Megan. To conceal her embarrassment, she turned cool and aloof toward her mother. As her intellect continued to mature, she eyed her mother critically, comparing her to sophisticated career women. Megan's icy distance saddened her mother. Megan saw her mother's sad feelings as weakness, and instead of softening her heart, it fueled her harsh and poisonous thoughts.

What Megan didn't know was that conflict, ill-will, deceit, and negative feelings cover the golden love thread with a heavy, sticky substance, and interfere with the flow of good feelings.

One night Megan dreamed of being strangled and pulled back and forth by a heavy, dark chain. When she called out for help, an angelic being appeared and spoke lovingly to her. "You have created these chains and added this burden to your life. If you continue this way, you will attract people into your life who have the appearance you covet, and the deceit you try to hide. Your mother has more goodness and spiritual power in her little finger than all the people you envy put together." The angel showed her how the golden thread looked before she became critical of her mother, then let her see how her negative thoughts and feelings covered the once luminous thread with layer upon layer of thick, black tar.

The angel told her how to heal the relationship. "Take a moment each day and visualize yourself cleansing the golden thread in a shower of white light. You can also begin a journal, and write one thing each day—only the good—that you see in your mother. Do this with all people you love. This golden thread is real, and it keeps love fresh and alive."

Megan learned a lesson that has a message for each of us. When the beautiful heart threads become encrusted with a heavy, black substance, it interferes with the flow of love and good feelings. When this happens relationships become toxic. Each of us must decide how we want to connect with people. We can create clean ties that uplift and nourish us or indulge in negativity to drain and break us. If you decide that someone is worth keeping in your life, as Megan did with her mother, remember: It takes only a minute to begin to heal the golden threads of love. *Within each twenty-four hour cycle, cleanse the threads of love between yourself and those close to you. Do not overlook the importance of this daily practice. This is a significant step toward changing your energy flow and inner atmosphere.*

May the Blessings Be—On The Road

Something happens to people while driving in rush hour traffic; everyone is looking at everyone else as an annoyance, or an adversary, often cursing and muttering as they drive. These negative thoughts do not stay in the car. They poison the "inner atmosphere" and cause thought pollution! Remember: thoughts carry energy. It is your choice if your thoughts carry the power and energy to uplift or destroy. No wonder it's so difficult to see beyond our problems—thought pollution is obstructing our vision! To help clean up the "atmosphere," practice this exercise for one minute the next time you stop at a traffic light. Bless every car that passes and say to them, with a feeling of compassion, "May the blessings be. Have a safe trip on the road today!"

◆

Tim drove through traffic, swearing and wondering why everyone else was so stupid. "They never pay attention, they try to cut me off," he would mutter to himself, and his blood pressure would rise as he was driving.

One evening, he was out on a "first time date" with a woman named Gwen. Shocked by his fiery temper, she wondered if this was a danger signal alerting her to avoid this man. Gwen decided she'd give him a chance to respond differently.

She shared her "car blessing technique" with Tim, saying, "May the blessings be. Have a safe trip on the road today," to every passing vehicle. He thought this was ridiculous, but his strong attraction to Gwen influenced him to humor her and play along. They sat at each stop light, blessing cars, laughing together. A bus approached and Tim remarked, "I really hate those stinky buses; we don't have to bless them, do we?" "Absolutely," replied Gwen. Tim's temper gave a subtle flare, but he continued blessing cars and buses. He found it wasn't so difficult, because of Gwen's calming presence next to him. His personal atmosphere shifted, and Gwen felt her heart open.

By the time they arrived at the restaurant, he felt great and was thrilled that he didn't need his usual two martinis to feel relaxed. Tim continued dating Gwen, eventually married her, and found himself blessing cars even when he wasn't with her. Occasionally, he even shares this technique with other men and finds they are more open than he imagined. *So, the next time you stop at a traffic light and see people who seem to be sending you a blessing, send it right back!*

A Pure and Open Vehicle for Spiritual Healing

At times we may feel sad or helpless in a situation regarding a loved one who may be ill, in need of our love and support, or close to death. We may feel sad because they are separated from us and the distance is far. Remember, you can sit still and do something. You can learn to collapse the distance and be with those you love.

◆

Dawn has a much younger sister, Meriya, who was pregnant and afraid of the birth process. Because Dawn has been a source of strength and inspiration for Meriya, she requested that Dawn be with her at the birth. Dawn did not want the new child to enter the world surrounded by fear, yet the three-thousand-mile distance that separated the sisters presented a challenge.

Since childhood, Dawn has experienced the presence of spiritual beings protecting and guiding her life. She has triumphed over abandonment and struggles that few people know of and now she wanted to pass on this protection to her sister.

Some years ago she learned a spiritual practice but never had used it with a specific individual in mind until now. When the day came for Meriya to become a mother, Dawn found a quiet place to be alone. *This practice requires the purest of intentions.* You sit quietly and go to that sacred place within yourself. Dawn focused on a column of pure white light that started as a pinpoint a few inches above her head. She surrounded herself with this light until a powerful sound current enveloped and permeated her whole being. Filled with devotion for God, she spoke, *"I declare myself a pure and open vehicle for Divine Spirit."* A blissful nectar flowed from the center of her being and filled her personal atmosphere. She then invited her sister and the child to enter the radiant circle. Once Meriya entered circle, Dawn requested that she be protected and free of fear for the duration of her birthing. She asked that the baby receive blessings from the spiritual beings who protected her when she was a child.

The next day Meriya telephoned, delighted with her birthing experience. The baby was a boy; his name is Randy. She felt no fear and wondered if an angel watched over her. *You can practice this act of love when you feel concern about those you care for deeply.*

Awaken to Moments of Compassion

*It's easy to excel in the "theory of spiritual principles."
The challenge is putting into practice what we've read and
heard, especially in family life. It is at home that we often
meet our most trying tests and have the greatest opportunity for growth. Here is one of my own "One-Minute
Healing Experiences."*

◆

After one hour in a yoga class, back in the summer
of 1968, I was hooked. The ordinary-looking room at
the YWCA in Utica, New York, became a shrine for
me. The teacher's soothing voice instructed us to "do
our best, and turn our focus inward." That meant no
one could evaluate the size of my breasts or thighs.
The subdued lighting increased my confidence. My
nonathletic body liked yoga. I was able to gracefully
glide in and out of the postures, feeling more like a
swan than an ugly duckling. No competition, and no
teams to be chosen—what bliss!

Yoga involved the body, mind, and spirit. For
someone who much preferred to be reading Plato or
Pythagoras rather than running around the track
(reading anything, even *Cosmopolitan* magazine, was
preferable to running)—this was a dream come true.
I could say I was exercising, think about the myster-
ies of the universe, and not be criticized for it!

After six months of classes, I headed off to a weekend yoga retreat. We ate vegetarian food with our fingers, practiced yoga postures and deep breathing, and learned that the purpose of yoga was to gain inner peace and awareness of the Divine Source through meditation, breathing, ethics, and postures. It was emphasized that anyone from any religious (or nonreligious) background could practice yoga by embracing the essence of the yogic philosophy—peace, integrity, clarity, and compassion.

Upon returning home (I was eighteen and still living with my parents), I overheard my mother explaining my yoga experience to one of our relatives. "She goes to see the God of yoga, where they lay on the floor with their legs up, instead of kneeling down to pray. She won't eat meatballs or pepperoni anymore, but I don't think she's lost any weight." Infuriated, I wondered if she was awake when I gave her the definition for Hatha Yoga: HA means Sun, THA means Moon, and it is the uniting of opposing forces of the body, mind, and spirit? I was about to scream that she had everything wrong and tangled up as usual, when I felt an inner nudge to be calm, and then I remembered the essence of the weekend: *Truth that cannot be spoken in love and inward peace is not truth.*" My mother prayed that I would stop correcting and trying to change her, and that I would convert to her version of "niceness." Yoga was the beginning of my personal spiritual odyssey and helped answer my mother's prayers in a way she never expected. *Wherever your journey begins, open yourself to wisdom that fills you with greater compassion.*

One-Minute Healing Meditations

Extend your goodwill and COMPASSION to every being in the universe. Let go of hate, envy, and adversarial positioning. For one moment, lift your spirit to meet all people, all animals, and all life as companions.

◆

Too many people seeking spiritual awakening want more and more "phenomena" and run in dozens of directions looking for the source of "energy highs." If you ask any electricians if it is possible to pump a large bolt of electricity through wiring before it is properly insulated and grounded, they'll laugh at you. Of course it's possible they'd say, "Sure, if you want to burn down your house or the whole neighborhood." Our bodies are like electrical systems. Before we can be "turned on" to receive more current, we must wire our hearts and minds to the Divine Spirit.

◆

lled with vitality, impregnate your emo-
hts and actions with love.

◆

A great misunderstanding has occurred over the centuries about the difference between human love and divine love. Most people crave the emotional rush that romantic love brings, and they evaluate relationships solely by that criteria. Others let special feelings of passion die and convince themselves they don't miss it at all. Some people have discovered it is possible to have both. What is important is to recognize this: physical love moves through cycles and seasons, but divine love is eternally blossoming. Divine love can heal all levels of your life.

◆

Spirit is love, that which binds all of us together. It is Spirit that brings about healing or change in an individual.

◆

Ask permission for what you want from the Earth. If you want to plant flowers or vegetables, ask the Earth, "I'd like permission." Begin now, in this moment, to treat the Earth with greater respect. We are visitors here, and the Earth has graciously provided for us. It is time to acknowledge the gifts we've received.

◆

Give evidence of your character in deeds of loving kindness.

◆

Choose an animal that comes to mind. Ask what gifts the animal is holding for you. Accept the gift with loving thanks. Now speak to the guardian angel of that animal species. Ask if there is any assistance you may provide to that animal group. Make a commitment to the guardian angel, by saying, "I treat all living creatures with love and respect."

◆

With a pure heart, look in the mirror and into the depth of your eyes!

◆

Visualize a child you love. It can be any child from the present, past, or future. Next, find your most beautiful feeling of Self and flow it out to the child unconditionally. Tell the child you do have time to listen.

◆

When you read about love and kindness, observe your emotional reaction. If you are quick to react with a strong emotion—either positive or negative—step back and ask yourself: What have I invested into my self-image that is being shaken?

Longevity &
Rejuvenation

Would you like to extend
your health span and fulfill your spiritual purpose? It
is possible. I started working with longevity and
rejuvenation practices in my twenties. The benefits
and blessings are certainly noticeable in my forties.

◆

If we could exactly duplicate
the state of consciousness of a healthy,
optimistic individual, we would cease our struggle
to copy their outer actions.

◆

Our consciousness includes everything we see, experience, believe, love, and value—on an emotional, mental, physical, and spiritual level. Health, wealth, beauty, and genius are manifested from our individual consciousness.

Instead of focusing on anti-aging foods and age-defying exercise routines, which are essential, let's explore the inner practices that influence outer behavior. What leads some of us toward healthy, living foods and into a stress-reducing yoga class, and what drives others down the depression path into addictions and apathy? Remember, it is the flow of our energy.

To create your own success story, start aiming to direct your energy flow upward, and turn on your inner light. You can stop struggling, without coming to a dead stop and stagnating. Once the inner light is activated, it will rejuvenate you as it shines more brightly on the pathways that hold your greatest potential.

Revise Your Thoughts Before You Sleep

Never carry sad or negative thoughts into your sleep and dream time. Practice this revision technique for one minute each night, and you could change your attitude, your energy, and erase years of stress.

◆

Bill had developed a draining habit; every night he carried his daily disappointments to bed with him. As soon as he shut his eyes and his head hit the pillow, he would mentally rehash his entire day. Criticizing himself for not saying the right thing to his clients and bullying himself for not negotiating the best deal were always his last thoughts before drifting to sleep. Come morning, he felt fatigued and wondered why eight or nine hours of sleep never seemed like enough.

Bill went to a homeopathic physician about his fatigue. The doctor was adept with much more than herbs and nutrition, and he questioned Bill in depth about his nightly rituals.

The doctor gave Bill this prescription: Each night when you get into bed, relax and take a few deep breaths. Close your eyes and review the portions of your day that bite and burn your insides. Mentally move beyond your fumbling, reticent self. Forgive yourself for missing the mark, and mentally transform yourself into your ideal. Embellish and exaggerate your virtues. Fill your last waking moments with positive images of yourself, and carry these thoughts into the inner world of dreams.

For example, see yourself in the midst of your failed business negotiations of that day, or any situation that brought bad news. Now, imagine yourself in that situation. As you walk into the room feeling strong and powerful, you see yourself communicating with the precision of an expert. Your associates recognize and value the depth of your knowledge and experience. They are thrilled to be associated with you. The deal is consummated with ease, and everyone walks out a winner. You knew you could do it, and you know you can do it again.

The doctor added a word of caution: *Never use this or any technique to create a "win" for yourself by deceiving or manipulating another.*

Within one month, Bill was comfortable with the revision technique. Each day he was awake a little earlier and feeling happier. With his extra time, he was working to gain more expertise in his field, and his nightly confidence was beginning to shine during the daylight. This type of revision doesn't cost anything, and you don't have to travel any farther than your bedroom to prove it to yourself.

Commit to Inner Music and Cheer

The power of thoughts, words, and images are very real and influence the world and those around you. If you are unhappy with the way people are responding to you, or have negative feelings about the area you live in, it may be time for inner music and cheer.

◆

Danny recalled the days when he loved living in New York, but his memory of happy times was fast fading. He noticed more callousness every day. People were living in their own thought prisons and the negativity thickened and became more solid everywhere he looked. He wondered if he was falling prey to the stereotypes about large, impersonal cities. Doesn't anyone ever say *please* or *thank you* anymore, and actually mean it? What about a sincere smile? These thoughts continued to chatter and chew at his mind, making him sad and sick.

One morning, Danny got up unusually early and saw a beautiful rainbow spanning the city. In that moment, he decided to make an all-out commitment to give more joy and sunshine to everyone who looked so weary, including himself. He began to say *thank you* and *please* and smile with his eyes and his mouth. He was discovering his lost enthusiasm. Only a few people responded, but rather than quit, he became more creative. An inner voice whispered encouragement, "It only takes a minute to be kind and cheerful."

He appointed himself "East Coast Distributor for Please, Thank You, and Smiling!" In his imagination he began placing golden balls and chimes above his head, as if he were accompanied by a magical marching band of invisible musicians. As he walked in and out of shops and stores, he noticed babies and small children waving at him. He imagined the chimes sparkling and playing music, and the children actually began to laugh aloud. Before long, adults were smiling at him and saying thank you! He realized that creativity extended far beyond the physical plane. As the days and weeks rolled by, life was changing for Danny and the people in his world—they all experienced a little more sunshine and music.

Enthusiasm and Confidence Are in Your Voice

Your tone of voice, pace, and speaking style can affect your attitude and the way others respond to you. You can command greater authority or lighten the mood, with your voice. Practice speaking in different tones, by reading aloud. Close your eyes when you watch TV or a movie. Can you guess the mood and age of the actors by their voices?

◆

Kevin was having difficulty relating to his new boss, Todd, who was fifteen years younger than Kevin. He was certain that he was doing everything right, and he'd never experienced a problem with his previous boss. Kevin observed Todd with other guys his age, and they seemed to be doing fine.

One morning Todd called Kevin into his office. "Kevin, you are long overdue for a promotion. Your work is excellent, but management hasn't rewarded you. Do you know why?" Kevin was shocked to learn that Todd thought he deserved a promotion. He worked for the phone company for eleven years and gave no thought to promotions going to others. Todd continued, "I think it could be the way you speak. Your voice is so soft, and you express your thoughts in a hesitating manner. Most people associate a slow, uncertain speaking voice with a lack of youthful energy and low self-esteem. You sound much older and weaker than you are."

Kevin just stared at Todd. "Well," he said, "I'm not going to start shouting." "Of course not," replied Todd. "But you could learn to vary the rate of your speech, and the tone, to show more confidence and enthusiasm. You've heard the commonly used phrases 'drained and empty,' or 'buoyant and up-lifted,' haven't you? Your voice places you at one end or the other of that spectrum. Move yourself toward the center, where you'll feel solid and confident."

Bewildered, Kevin didn't have a clue where to begin. Todd continued, "All you need to do is spend one minute each evening reading aloud. Experiment until you are comfortable picking up the pace and adding a little volume to the words you want to emphasize. Read anything aloud, even the newspaper will do, to start."

Feeling silly at first, Kevin began to practice reading aloud. He kept at it but wasn't sure it made any difference. Three months passed, and an amazing thing happened. Several of Kevin's co-workers cornered him, saying, "You seem like you've dropped ten years; what's going on, do you have a new girlfriend?" Todd was standing nearby, smiling, and approached the group. "I know Kevin's secret; he's the new department supervisor! I'm sure he has a waiting list of women who want to go out and celebrate with him!"

The Temple of Inner Silence

Any person who is able to have one full moment of silence, free of nagging disruptions in the mind, could easily begin to break free from addictions to drugs, alcohol, gambling, food, or any situation that is abusive. Alcohol, drugs, and all varieties of addictions thrive in a noisy, cluttered mind. Once you have become adept at entering into Silence, let yourself be filled with love flowing from the heart of God.

◆

The lifestyle of a musician is like a double-edged sword. Along with creativity and excitement come the traps of abuse in all forms—constant travel, free drinks, and drugs, and night-long parties with delicious looking women. Some may say, "Well, that ain't so bad," and would gladly trade it for the routine of their lives. However, Father Time and the Lords of Karma have a way of catching up with us when our actions lack balance.

John was performing with his band at a "gentlemen's" topless bar, and walking along the sharp edge of the sword. Rich men dressed in Italian wool and silk were the clientele. After eight nights of parties with the elite of the city, he met an unusual man who sat next to him on his 2:00 AM break. His piercing blue eyes attracted John's attention. "Just call me Blue," he smiled. John sat with him, and they discussed their views on life.

Blue asked, "What are your plans for the future?" John replied, "What do you mean?" Blue asked again. John said, "Do you mean money? I've got some stashed." Again, Blue asked the same question, ignoring John's response. Instead of feeling uncomfortable, John opened up and replied, "Gee, I never really thought about where I was going in my life."

Blue said, "Take a good look around; what do you see?" After scanning the bar and dance area, John took a deep breath and replied, "I see lonely, unhappy people, hiding from life." He grinned and added, "After a few drinks, they look a lot better." Blue laughed and said, "How is it you can be so perceptive at seeing through this illusion of happiness, and yet you wallow in it every night."

John responded defensively, "Look at you, what are you doing in here?" Blue confidently replied, "Helping you—but only if you want the help." John pondered and looked around at his surroundings again. "Well, maybe I do need some help, talk on."

"There is a law in physics that goes like this: No two things can occupy the same space at the same time. With this principle in mind, work on one unwanted habit at a time, say drinking, drugs, or promiscuity. Every time you have a craving for one of your addictions, replace the feeling of the craving with these steps: First, take several deep breaths and still yourself. Second, begin to sing the word: HU. If you are alone, sing aloud. Otherwise do this in silence. This is one of the sacred words that charges your atmosphere with wisdom, compassion and power. It can be chanted as H-U, or as HUGH. Continue this practice for several minutes. Listen with your inner ears and eventually you will hear a soft, soothing humming, or perhaps the powerful roaring of the sea. Allow the sound to move inside your stomach, then invite it to move upward to your heart, and upward again into your throat and head, until it fills and permeates your entire being. If you have difficulty hearing with your inner ears, don't be concerned. Just breathe deeply, slowly, listening to the sound of your breath as it rises and falls, and continue to sing: HU.

In the beginning, you may struggle with ten or twenty seconds of deep, healing silence. When your heart becomes ripe with the sweet nectar of the sound, the door to the inner temple opens instantly. This is where all healing begins. If you hear musical sounds, perhaps the single note of a flute or violins, that is wonderful, as long as your heart remains open. *It is important that silence precedes the light and sound. Silence cleanses the mind and begins to break the attachment to the draining and debilitating traps of life.* When you've mastered this, pick another limiting condition and continue the healing process."

John closed his eyes for a few seconds to absorb what he'd heard. When he looked up, ready to say "thank you," Blue was gone, leaving John to ponder what he had seen and heard that night.

Musical Healing

Select music to listen to that expresses the mood you would like to be in, not the mood you are in now. Music has a tremendous rejuvenating power. Most people do not realize that music can move us spiritually, mentally, emotionally, and physically, and influence the way we act.

◆

After an exhausting week at work, Marie looked forward to a day at the beach. She intended to get out of the house early on Saturday and break her habit of spending so much time in isolation. Plus, she was tired of her friends teasing her about always being late. She turned on the popular music she always listened to, and its heartbreaking melodies filled her with longing. She poked around the kitchen, and then looked out the window. The lyrics from one song after another echoed a similar theme of love betrayed and lost. Several hours later, she wondered what happened to her morning. Late as usual, she felt so depressed that she decided to stay home. As the day dragged on, she felt worse and wondered what she could do. She'd read everything possible on procrastination, but nothing worked. She turned on the television and heard a discussion about changing your mood and attitude through using music.

The next morning, Marie put on an upbeat salsa instead of the familiar heartbreaking melodies. She felt jazzed and quickly got into the shower. The music played on, and Marie was dressed and out the door in the most effortless way. It turned out to be her best day off in months! Everywhere she went, she met cheerful people who seemed to be inwardly dancing to a lively musical beat.

That evening she arranged her music collection by mood. Soft, soothing pieces were ready to play after a tense day at work. Broadway hits were great for bringing on laughter or romance. Since she now understood the power of music, she said good-bye to some of the pieces that drained her energy. She set up several mood-changing categories, and over the years she has shared this with many friends. Marie always knows she has the right music for the right mood when she can see and feel a positive change within herself in just one minute.

Creating A Healing Atmosphere

Your home could rejuvenate you each day, after you return from the stress you meet in the world. The love and spiritual vibrations filling each room can relieve your tension and invisible stress. For years, I wished for a home that would be my own "healing center"—a place of beauty, serenity, and magic. Dreams come true in ways we least imagine. Here is how it happened for me.

◆

A few years ago, I moved into my dream house. On the day I moved in, I walked from room to room, smiling, and my heart pushed at my chest. Everywhere I looked, the turquoise-blue colors created a mood to make me feel as if I were in a temple in ancient Greece or Egypt. It didn't matter how my home looked to an interior designer, or to a more worldly person. In my home, I feel ageless and time-less.

During the first week in my new home, I un-packed box after box, but instead of frustration, I felt exhilaration. More than half the boxes were filled with books, and I considered waiting before starting that project, knowing it could take days. I tore open a box of kitchen items, and sitting on top of forks and spoons was a book. I picked it up, and a white card fell to the floor. Scribbled in my own handwriting on the card, were the words, *"Large white house with windows everywhere, looking out at the water."* I walked to the window, holding the card, and glanced out over the serene blue lake. My new-found friend, a beautiful white swan, floated toward me.

That card survived eight years and several moves. It was written during a Wishcraft Seminar given by Barbara Sher in New York City. Barbara encouraged us to follow our enthusiasm and wish for whatever we wanted, even if it seemed totally im-practical and out of reach. I fantasized about living in a "healing center" on the water. Barbara Sher ex-plained how to look beyond material objects and delve into the "keystone" and the feeling at the core of the wish. The feeling I wanted involved serenity, spaciousness, and magic. I didn't have to struggle to create an image and feeling of what I wanted, and this helped reveal one of my true goals.

At the time I attended the seminar, I lived on Long Island. Although there were plenty of waterfront houses, they cost plenty of money, and that was what I didn't have. Over the years, I continued to feel myself living in a large white house on water, filling myself with feelings of floating swans and flying unicorns. I didn't have a clue how I'd ever get it, because prices just kept climbing.

When I moved to Las Vegas, I forgot all about living on the water and was at least thankful for sunshine and good friends. One morning I drove out of the city, beyond the glitter of the Las Vegas hotels, looking for a house. My body shivered at the sight of a peaceful blue lake, surrounded by palm trees, in a community called Desert Shores. Gracefully floating in the lake were the swans of my dreams. Beyond the lake stood the rainbow-colored mountains. In one moment, I knew I'd found my home!

The story of how I was able to afford and move into the house could fill another book of miracles. Looking out of my window each morning, I know I have found my "healing center." My home rejuvenates me each time I enter the door; it is the small piece of heaven I longed for.

The atmosphere we live in has great importance and is shaped by the activities that we pursue. A wise teacher made this comment: *"The thoughts emanating from your mind produce rays. These rays pass into the atmosphere through your outgoing breath and saturate your heart, your cells, and your environment. This is why people make journeys to visit sacred places. Sacred places that have been visited by saints and spiritual beings are saturated with powerful healing waves. It is good to ask what kind of waves prevail in your home."*

Wherever your home may be today, begin to fill yourself with feelings and images of your personal healing center. You can create a "sacred" place of healing and upliftment in your home. The rejuvenation process begins as soon as you anchor your heart and mind to living in a space that is ageless, timeless, and divine.

One-Minute Rejuvenating Meditations

Sit quietly and touch the place between and slightly above your eyebrows. Visualize a doorway in the place between your eyes. As you move your hand away from your forehead, the door opens. Look through the door for some form of Light, and listen with your inner ears for words of encouragement and guidance.

◆

Snowball technique: Imagine you are gathering up all your unwanted thoughts, feelings, and circumstances, and placing them into a large, white snow-ball. Use your hands and make the motions to tightly pack the snowball. Now, visualize a powerful, golden river flowing by you. Stand up and inhale as you lift the snowball. Toss the snowball effortlessly into the river. Exhale deeply as soon as the snowball falls into the river, and watch it rapidly dissolve as it flows away from you.

◆

Lie on the floor for a deep-breathing break. If you're not alone, encourage your family and friends to join you. Close your eyes, and place your fingers three inches below your navel. Begin the breathing from this point. Inhale slowly, filling your stomach with air, like an expanding balloon. Breathe slowly and deeply, and feel the sides and top of your stomach expand. This is one time you don't need to worry whether your stomach looks huge! Continue inhaling until you fill your chest and finally feel your collarbone lift. Exhale at the same slow, rhythmic pace. Repeat three times.

◆

When you are outdoors in pleasant weather, find a quiet place to lie down and feel the steadiness and stillness of the Earth. Steadiness and stillness are the essence of Mother Earth. Say to yourself, "I am as steady and still as a great mountain. No outside influence can topple me!" In your mind's eye, imagine a magnificent, towering mountain. Take a few deep breaths. As you inhale, fill each cell in your body with steadiness and stillness. With each exhalation, release all tension and anxiety, feeling it dissolve. Any time your life is shaking with uncertainty, lie down and experience the steadiness and stillness of the Earth, until you feel clearheaded.

◆

If the state of your health is not all that it could be, look at your thinking. Most important—do not blame yourself. Abandon critical thoughts that contain disease germs and bring a harvest of sickness, decay, weakness, and failure. Be compassionate and gentle with yourself and ask: What is the harvest to be?

◆

Take off your shoes and socks. (If this takes more than a minute you need to lose ten pounds and take a stretching class). Squeeze each toe gently, and give each toe a name. Name your little toe, "HANNABELL." Anytime later in the day that you have a problem to solve, ask Hannabell, "What shall I do?" Use your slowest, sexiest voice.

◆

Eat a blueberry.

◆

Find a soft, clean patch of green grass. Take off your shoes and socks. Ask permission of the Earth, saying, "I'd like to take a refreshing walk on the healing green grass." Wiggle your toes and feel your whole body, up to the top of your head, becoming energized with the vibrant, healing power of the Earth.

◆

Bitter, negative thoughts are energy drains. When you lapse into lamenting, visualize a toilet, and watch your energy being flushed away and lost. Then shift your focus, the way you change the TV channels, until you find a bubbling spring. Watch the water percolate up, and feel it as it bursts into action.

◆

Eat Less, Breathe More.

◆

Get your favorite drinking vessel and fill it with fresh pure water. Take very slow sips. With each sip, experience the water quenching your thirst and your desires. By the time you finish the glass of water, know that you already have all you want. It only takes your consistent acceptance of your new state for it to be.

◆

The ancient art of Chinese face-reading tells us: *"The face you have from birth to age twenty-five is the face your mother gave you. From twenty-five to fifty, you create your own face, and from fifty on, you have the face you deserve."*

Prosperity &
Abundance

If there is great abundance in the universe, and more than enough for everyone, why are so many people starving? Why are poverty and homelessness increasing? Why are so many afraid of the future?

One reason is that our individual life force and optimism have become pushed down and repressed. When the life force is anchored low and is so small it can fit in our baby toe, we see what is lacking, instead of looking for ways to attract abundance. *We have to fill every cell full of energy and light, and be alert and awake, so we can act on opportunity when it knocks at our door.*

There are many mixed messages about prosperity. Should we desire greater material wealth and indulge ourselves, or live simply to save the environment and our integrity? Here is a clue: there once was a man who asked a great sage why his material wealth failed to bring happiness. The reply: *Luxury and privilege are not ingredients in creating happiness. All you need is something to be enthusiastic about—something to look forward to. If you've lost your enthusiasm, neither simple living nor luxury will satisfy you.*

As long as we plant seeds that yield just enough to get by, there will be scarcity. We have to ask for a thousand times more light and love than we could ever imagine, to create enthusiasm, abundance, and prosperity. After you have asked for an abundance of light and love, be careful what else you ask for; you just might get it! *The best guideline to follow when asking for experiences or "things" is: Ask for whatever you are able to take care of and love.*

Occasionally, I find myself wishing for ten cats, a dozen swans, a tiger, a lion, and a bear. Even when I cut the list back to ten cats, I realize that I am not able to take care of them, and having them would drain the enthusiasm I felt when I first imagined them. Then I ask myself, what can I lovingly care for? As your wishes begin to come true, continue to feed and fuel your enthusiasm, because it attracts abundance.

One-Minute Inner Conversations

Our thoughts influence others to create prosperity and goodwill, or confusion and chaos. Others echo that which we whisper to them in silence.

◆

On his ride to work, Paul felt his anger swell because he dreaded going to his office. He owned a successful mortgage company but doubted whether he could continue working there much longer. His mind continued to replay the same distressing thoughts whenever he gave attention to the guys who worked with him. "They use the copy machine and leave me with no paper. They tie up the phone lines with frivolous calls. They eat like pigs and never bring in any food; they just devour everything in sight. The way they dress and the language they use is an embarrassment. Yet, they produce and bring in money. I left accounting because it was boring, and look at me! Do I have to give up a great income for peace of mind?"

Paul disliked confrontations and kept his frustration inside. Talking the situation over with his wife only made him feel worse. "Just ask them to be more polite," she said. He rolled his eyes as her sweet voice droned on and on.

Paul mentioned his dilemma to his friend, Mitch. "Do you talk to them mentally?" Mitch asked. Paul admitted that every morning on his way to work, his anger felt like black bile in his mouth. He spewed his anger toward them as he drove, using words he would never speak aloud.

Mitch helped Paul realize this: *We each have mental conversations, and when these conversations are critical and harsh, they intensify a negative situation instead of making it better.*

Paul mistakenly believed he was relieving his frustrations. Instead of improving the situation, this draining habit multiplied his problems. Paul agreed to begin one-minute mental conversations before he got to the office, and to use only positive words and images. He mentally talked to his co-workers about an environment filled with "good vibes" and prosperity. He inwardly stated his intentions with strength and clarity. He began to praise them, mentally and aloud, for small improvements. Within a few months, the office atmosphere had transformed into a true community of team players. A few people left, and new people, who wanted to be part of a successful team, became part of the company. Paul found his income climbing, and the harmony in the office was tangible to everyone.

Happy Pinball of Enthusiasm

For those of us who believe that consciousness constructs our reality, enthusiasm can fuel any endeavor we genuinely have a passion to achieve.

◆

Morale among employees was at an all-time low. The exterior appearance of the upscale department store sparkled with success, but an undercurrent of fear dominated behind the scenes. Sales continued to drop, and the employees were whining and bickering. Management ruled with an "iron hand." The store manager talked down to everyone, reprimanding them constantly. Apathy set in, due to continual blame and threats because of poor sales.

Melissa was a recent hire in the cosmetics department. She was one of fifty-five sales associates, and she noticed the negative atmosphere spreading beyond their department. She knew it was useless to speak with management. After all, who would listen to the new kid on the block? Instead, she took action and devised a plan. First, she got to work early and took the time to make sure her area was spotless. She expressed genuine interest in each person and smiled to show she cared. Customers gravitated to her. In just one short month, Melissa was the top salesperson in the department.

Some of her co-workers began to notice and liked being around her. Others were jealous and envious. The negatives did not bother Melissa. She persisted with her enthusiasm and continued to show there was no lack, only abundance. Over the days and weeks, a few of her co-workers asked how she maintained such an optimistic attitude. What was her secret? Melissa said, "If you truly want to know and learn the secret, I'll show you; however, you must be sincere." Several sincere co-workers agreed to meet with Melissa.

Melissa told the group, *"Enthusiasm is the secret! Enthusiasm is infectious!"* One of the women responded, "That may be easy for you, but I've never been enthusiastic; it's not my style." Melissa replied, "You have a good point. Phony enthusiasm annoys everyone, and it is more apparent than most people think. *Consider this: Enthusiasm goes far beyond style. We all have it hidden within, and internal stress often short-circuits the electricity of enthusiasm."*

Melissa continued, "If you want to set your enthusiasm free, it requires a little imagination and a change in atmosphere. For several years I aimed to increase my enthusiasm. Immediately after my daily meditation practice, while I was still in a state of deep peace and clarity, I would take a few moments to fill myself with enthusiasm. Sitting with my eyes closed, I would silently say the word *ENTHUSIASM*, until I could *feel* the essence of enthusiasm and the word became filled with a vibrant life force. I would visualize a bright, shiny ball, such as one you would use playing a pinball machine. Imagine this ball bouncing in your body, ricocheting and lighting up all the happy, positive qualities that lie within you. Bounce it off your heart, light it up; bounce it off your eyes, light them up; bounce it off your thoughts, and light them up."

The group began meditating and practicing the "pin ball" technique, while focusing on the word *ENTHUSIASM*. Anytime anyone would appear to be down, other members of the group would "snap their fingers" to remind them of the bright, shiny ball. Sales went up. More and more of their fellow co-workers were gravitating toward the "pinball" group. So much enthusiasm was flowing throughout the store that upper management took notice. They noticed because "bottom line" sales were soaring. What was going on, they wondered?

The president of the company visited the store, and he questioned one of the employees. "Why is everyone so happy and energetic?" "We all belong to the 'pinball' group," was her reply. "I don't understand," he said. She immediately introduced him to Melissa. The president invited Melissa upstairs to tell her success story to his personal corporate office staff. Melissa told them she refused to work in a place where she was not happy and productive. "There is no such thing as a lack of abundance, and I refuse to let apathy and fear rule my life. I simply applied my formula for living life to the fullest. *Live life with enthusiasm! Consider enthusiasm. Really think about it. Let it roll around the mind like a happy pinball, lighting up emotions and thoughts. Enthusiasm. For if variety is the spice, enthusiasm is the spice rack.*

Melissa now works at corporate headquarters as executive assistant to the president. We can support enthusiastic people, like Melissa, by paying attention to the atmosphere of every business we encounter. *If you want more enthusiasm in your life, get involved with this practice for 30 days, it is foolproof.*

Planting The Seeds of Miracles

When you have a deep, unshakable inner knowing that you will be taken care of, outer circumstances will match that inner state. This involves much more than repeating words or affirmations, although that is a good way to plant seeds of "knowing." Once the seeds have ripened and bear fruit, you reap the rewards of your own harvest. Here is one more miracle that came into my life.

♦

On my thirtieth birthday, I found myself at the end of a six-year marriage. My previous attempts to leave the relationship failed. This time I was determined to make a clean break. The only problem was a lack of funds—my savings amounted to $300.

I was too embarrassed to call my parents and ask for help. They knew I'd been earning good money and would have asked a hundred questions. I phoned my best friend, Mary Jean. She lovingly invited me to share her small, one-bedroom apartment. Fortunately, I was debt-free and my car was paid for. I drove from Las Vegas to Los Angeles, leaving my cats behind, until I could afford to take them with me.

Mary Jean worked in Beverly Hills for a management company that handled celebrities. On my second day with her, she said she'd heard that comedian Flip Wilson was looking for an assistant. "Go out and get that job!" she encouraged. I dialed the number, the phone rang three times, and Flip answered. "I'd like to be your assistant," I told him. He laughed and responded, "I never answer this phone; maybe you are meant to work for me."

The next morning I drove down La Cienega Boulevard, heading toward Flip's office. A red Porsche pulled in front of me. As I got closer to the Porsche, I could see the license plate. For a few seconds I felt as if I was in the "twilight zone" as I read: FLIP. I followed behind the red car until I arrived at the office address for my interview. Flip got out of his

Porsche. I got out of my Volkswagen. We looked at each other and shared a moment of deep recognition.

I followed him into his elegantly decorated suite of offices. He turned on the stereo and sat down. He closed his eyes as the theme from "Music Man" filled the room. After several minutes, he opened his eyes. "You're not uncomfortable with me, are you?" "No," I replied. "That's great," he continued. "If you want the job, call my accountant. Tell him you're on the payroll, starting today. Next week, we leave for a show I'm doing in Honolulu. You'll travel with my make-up and wardrobe people." I closed my eyes for a few seconds and inwardly sent the biggest wave of appreciation I could create out into the universe, saying, *"Thank you—big time!"*

As we were leaving the office, my new employer paused and held out his hand. He was wearing a ring that said "FLIP." He turned his hand over, and the back side of the ring said, "GOD." "That's who I work for," he announced. "I guess that's who you work for, or you wouldn't be here."

Instead of being amazed by all of this, it seemed completely natural to me—as if this was the way events were supposed to flow! That night I celebrated with Mary Jean, knowing that her love for me helped attract this moment of magic. Within a matter of weeks, I saved enough money to rent a place of my own. As it happened, an apartment in the same building with Mary Jean became available that week.

Working for Flip was like attending the "university of abundance and success." I am certain that my trust in always being taken care of magnetized this miracle into my life.

One-Minute Meditations on Prosperity and Abundance

With each breath we draw, we can live more abundantly. Our INTENT is of primary importance, because *intention directs the flow of your attention.* Without abundantly directed attention, you can achieve only the results that everyone else achieves—that is, a supply equal to the demand.

◆

Should you desire to be other than what you are, you can create an ideal of the type of person you want to be and assume the virtues and character of that person. An old metaphysical principle states: If you will hold this assumption in mind until it becomes a dominant feeling, the attainment of your ideal is inevitable.

◆

Your originating intentions and thoughts create their own hell or their own heaven-like circumstances and conditions. Your experiences are nothing less than your own choices and thoughts made visible.

◆

Clearly AFFIRM what you want. Be precise and specific. *Every sentence and phrase, whether we say it aloud, or quietly to ourselves is an affirmation. Affirmations aren't just special phrases you say when you have a goal—we all make affirmations every time we speak.* The most powerful affirmations contain words that have great significance to you. And, remember: strong, clear, genuine feeling makes a more powerful affirmation, whether it is positive or negative.

◆

You have unlimited free will in choosing your assumptions and thoughts, but no power to determine conditions and events. You can create nothing, but your assumption determines what portion of creation you will experience.

◆

Give thanks for all you have and all that is on its way to you. Make a fierce affirmation: *"I am on sched-*

ule to fulfill my destiny and purpose." Then, personalize
the statement. *"I am on schedule to . . . (let love into my
life) . . . (become a millionaire) . . . (get my pilot's license)
. . . (live in a healthy, strong body) . . . (receive the light of
God here and now)."*

◆

You can make a money magnet of yourself, but to
do so you must first consider how you can create
money and prosperous conditions for other people.

◆

Genuine enthusiasm is such a rare commodity
that we have become a society constantly craving
something new to excite us—just to create a little
enthusiasm. Look at the vast number of people who
are heavily in debt because they are addicted to
shopping, just to have a moment with something
new. *To create enthusiasm without going broke, focus on
what is new inside of you, what is blossoming and grow-
ing.*

◆

People constantly say they want a "new figure," a
"new love," a "new career," or "better health," and
they talk about it as if they are approaching a mos-
quito hunt in a jungle swamp. Their tone of voice,

facial expressions, and eyes say what the mouth denies. *Be congruent if you want success with affirmations.*

◆

Everything we get comes to us by the law of attraction. A prosperous thought cannot live in a consciousness of scarcity.

Wisdom &
Responsibility

Attempting to heal ourselves without wisdom is not only foolish, it is dangerous. Several years ago my mother phoned me and asked me what "karma" meant. I asked where she heard it, and she replied, "On the radio. Willie Nelson was singing and he said, 'The karma goes round and round.'" I told her it meant, "As you sow, so shall you reap."

"Well," she replied with a soft, sad voice, "I must have lived a very foolish life to have created so much suffering for myself. I've always been honest, loving, and kind, but I guess that's not enough."

I'd heard similar comments before—actually, hundreds of times before, while I worked presenting

seminars on personal growth and spiritual unfoldment. *But, this was my mother.* I knew she was telling
the truth—she didn't have a mean bone in her body;
she didn't know how to lie.

In that moment, I saw what could happen when
wisdom is ignored. My mother felt bitter and resent-
ful, and she possessed a stack of solid evidence to
back her up. "Why," she wondered, "should she look
at life with gratitude?" I told her it was not too late to
recapture the awe and wonder she once experienced
and reverse the downward pull of negativity. If gratitude was too much to consider, I suggested, she
could just begin to praise herself for little things and
slowly halt her harsh self-criticism.

She called me a few weeks later and surprised me
with her insight. "If you make emotional love your
only master, but you have neglected the truth that
was glaring at you from every direction, you will be
miserable. Wisdom comes to those who have the
boldness to ask for truth, the humility and gratitude
to recognize it when it arrives, and the courage to
take action." All I could say to her was, *"THANK
YOU!"*

Seek Out and Honor Your Own Path

*Taking a path to healing just because it has worked for
others may result in frustration and disappointment. Find*

and honor your own path. Ask if you are on the path that is right for you. If it takes more than one minute to receive an answer, open your mind and heart to new possibilities.

◆

Tony was healthy and financially successful, but negative thoughts plagued him and kept him awake at night. His gorgeous wife loved him, and he was still turned on to her after fifteen years of marriage. He didn't have addiction problems, and ninety percent of the population would have traded in all their good karma to take his place.

Reluctantly, he began therapy and found he was restless and bored in every session. He changed therapists six times in three years, feeling that this was not the place for him to heal, but he didn't know what else to do. He continued to ask inwardly, "Is this the right place for me to be?" He never got a clear yes, but he didn't want to be a quitter.

One afternoon he said to the therapist, *"Look, can't you just analyze me the way a mechanic looks at a car, give me an estimate on how long it takes to fix the damage, tell me the cost, and let me decide if I want to do this?"* They both burst into laughter, and the atmosphere in the room changed. Fortunately, his therapist recognized that Tony wasn't getting what he needed from traditional therapy, and rather than hold onto him, lovingly set him free. On the advice of the therapist,

Tony started acupuncture treatments, and his depression dissolved after three sessions! He continues to see the acupuncturist for "tune-ups." His nights became peaceful and his days meaningful. He remained friends with the therapist and told everyone who would listen about his *"One-Minute Healing Experience."*

Above You, Below You, To Your Right and Your Left

Throughout the day and into the night, observe the silent messages and thought-patterns you send to others. Thoughts are things! Close your eyes and visualize yourself sitting in a chair. Now, review the people and experiences you want in your life. Place a visual image and a feeling about the positive events and people on top of your head, on both sides of your body, and underneath the chair. Allow the feeling to linger for one minute.

◆

Michelle could sniff out negative people and experiences, and she barricaded the door when she saw them coming. The wanna-bes of the world were not in her address book. She was a rare person—when she gave her word, she kept it. When she said no, she meant it. Eating a tuna fish sandwich with a close friend held more meaning for her than nibbling caviar on a yacht with a bore, and she had done both!

She worked so hard to keep negative experiences out of her life, she couldn't understand why she continued to attract them. *She gave so much attention to what she didn't want, that she magnetized it to herself!* She continued to push the toxic people out of her life, only to find a new one turning up at work, or moving into the condo right next door.

One morning after a therapeutic massage, she told her situation to the masseuse. The masseuse asked her to stay on the table for a few minutes longer and explained how to put the images you want around yourself. "Visualize yourself sitting on a chair and placing the image of positive people (or good health, or whatever you want to attract) on top of your head, underneath your chair, and to the left and right. Be sure to include the feelings you want to experience. The more natural your feelings are, the closer you are to success. In other words, if you feel worried or anxious, it won't work."

Being relaxed after the massage helped create the right atmosphere to use the technique. Before one minute passed, Michelle jumped up from the table. *"I'm always seeing the negative people around me, and telling them to get out!"* In just one minute, Michelle saw how she attracted toxic people. It didn't take long for her to experience positive changes in her life, because she understood how to place her attention on what she wanted, instead of battling what she didn't want.

Reversing the Downward Spin

Most people lack the balanced, harmonious energy flow needed to "turn on" the inner light, magnetize moments of healing, and rebound from disappointment and illness. Becoming aware of the downward spin of energy and reversing the flow is the essence of powerful medicine for the soul.

◆

Like many of the baby boomers living in the 1990s, Chris attended dozens of personal growth seminars. He was certain he gained new insights as a result, but his inner calm could easily blow-up during daily disruptions. He observed many people who claimed to be "beyond anger," but he believed they were repressing their feelings. "When you are so angry that you want to scream and rage, should you smother that anger?" he wondered.

Chris read and reread the statement: "Energy flows where attention goes," yet he knew he was missing some essential part of this message. "If only I could see energy, then I might be able to master this," he thought. Contradictory information about emotions, feelings, and energy filled his head. He knew he wanted to be true to himself, but how? He came across a book that explained that feelings are like flowing water that can sustain life as it feeds and nourishes farmlands and forests. That water can rage in flooding torrents, destroying the food and life it once nourished, or it can stagnate in a swamp. He realized that his feelings did all of those things.

The day after reading this, he started his morning with happy, positive feelings. His first business appointment of the day went smoothly. He arrived an hour early for his second appointment, which was unusual for him. He was starting to feel even better when his cellular phone rang, and a client from out of town announced that she was at his office—without an appointment—and she wanted to know how quickly he could meet her. Feelings of panic started to flood his stomach and chest. "What is wrong with people; can't they ever call ahead—but I have to act charming toward her or I'll never be able to earn a living." As he flung that thought out into his personal atmosphere, it created the first opening for the negative energies to start their downward pull. He continued on to the next negative thought: "I don't know why I left my office to show a house to this new client; they won't buy anything—probably another confused, first-time buyer, wasting my time." The negative current was becoming stronger, and he placed another thought into the web. "I am so stupid to stay in the real estate business and have new agents work for me—not one of them is in the office when I really need them." The spin of energy was now circling in a downward, draining spiral, and Chris was feeling sick and anxious.

His phone rang again; this time it was his wife. "I just called to say I love you." Chris listened and thought it was uncanny that she phoned at this moment. He opened his heart, and the moment of love dissolved the negative web. Chris sensed the energy in his stomach and chest as it started to clear. Once the energy was moving upward again, he realized that he could have stopped building the negative web after the first or even second thought. His inner light was often snuffed out by the force of his negative feelings. He began to understand that he didn't have to see energy, because he could feel it in his body. His personal atmosphere was tangible!

When he arrived home, he shared his excitement with his wife: "For years I've been trapped by my own negativity, but I thought it was normal because everyone seems to live this way. Today I saw myself build a web that became a suffocating prison. I'm going to stop feeding my precious energy to those dangerous thoughts, because I want spiritual freedom. Maintaining inner calm and internalizing life-affirming thoughts into my personal atmosphere is the key. This may be only the first step, but I am committed to making choices that advance me toward the light."

The Moment to Move On in Spiritual Responsibility

Practicing spiritual disciplines is a beginning stage of purifying the heart and mind. Anyone who believes spiritual discipline is unimportant is deluded. Anyone who believes it can be practiced without loving kindness and spiritual maturity is creating a vacuum, not a spiritual sanctuary.

◆

I started investigating spiritual disciplines when I was nineteen, about three months before my first husband was killed in Vietnam. After his death, I immersed myself into these practices. Each day I read and studied sacred scriptures and spent at least an hour doing a spiritual contemplation exercise involving sacred chanting. I gave up all use of drugs, alcohol, tobacco, and caffeine. I aimed to rid myself of obstacles to enlightenment—lust, anger, greed, vanity, and attachment.

After five years of consistent practice, I believed I was living a disciplined spiritual life, when I discovered that my efforts accomplished much less than I had believed. A woman friend, Linda, stayed in my apartment visiting me for a few days while her husband, who was a musician, was traveling. I liked her gentle and good company and invited her to stay anytime. I rarely invited anyone to stay with me, as I found most people were not "pure enough," but Linda was like an angel. It was easy for me to keep my attention on God when she was around. We often did spiritual practices together and stayed up late into the night discussing books and ideas.

After the third visit with me, Linda walked into the kitchen and burst into tears. As I tried to soothe her, she confided that the atmosphere in my home made her uncomfortable. Shocked by this, I asked if she could explain what was wrong. I worked to keep negative thoughts out of my mind and felt confused by her distress. "You don't know how to take care of your friends." Still bewildered, I asked for more information. "You go about living just as you do when you are alone. You have never asked what kind of food I like. You just offer me what you eat. You've never made a special meal—just brown rice, granola, and fruit—every visit is the same." She continued, and as I listened I knew this was about much more than food. I realized I was so self-absorbed in my "spiritual practices" and "disciplines" that I could not feel anything beyond my own silly nose. In my attempts to move beyond a conventional life filled with negative emotions, I created a sterile shrine to myself.

Linda taught me a powerful lesson: If I didn't know how to pay attention and care for a spiritual friend, what did I really know about welcoming

Divine Spirit into my life. She was a vehicle for teaching me that a sanctuary and a spiritual atmosphere require much more than discipline over negative thinking and behavior. I began to see that practicing spiritual discipline was like sending your application off before entering college—it was an important, yet very beginning step toward an education.

At that point—about twenty-five years ago—I did not have the balanced, harmonious energy flow needed to "turn on" my inner light, and magnetize moments of healing into our friendship. Fortunately, I was not devastated by the experience. I knew I would have other opportunities to experience that balanced, harmonious flow with Linda, and with others—and my knowing was true.

Ask in Silence—Be Willing to Hear the Truth

When you experience a strong emotion, ask a question, then be totally still. Wait for a clear thought, idea, or feeling to surface. You must be willing to know the truth to get clear answers. Take one minute several times throughout your day to ask, relax, be still, then let go.

◆

In 1980, I was living in Los Angeles, and I began to have feelings of fear and images of crashing cars each time I drove on the freeways. The traffic in Los Angeles was terrible, but this was an irrational anxiety. It was a sharp panic that started so suddenly, it shocked me.

This was strange and out of character for me. I confidently handled myself on icy roads in upstate New York from age seventeen and have driven myself across country more than once. Each time the wave of fear entered my mind, I pushed it away, affirming that I was confident and safe. The feelings came for a few weeks, then would leave for several months, only to return again. There was no unusual stress in my life that I could attribute this feeling to. I used every affirmation I knew of, yet nothing worked. Whenever the anxiety and fear crawled into my mind, I chased it out, telling the fear to return to its source.

Two years later, on a dark, rainy night, I was with my husband, Tom, in Vermont. He was driving us home to Long Island after a holiday weekend. Out of the darkness came a drunk driver, speeding and out of control. I saw the car heading directly for us, and then everything went white. When I regained consciousness, my leg was numb and wouldn't move. The crash was so devastating, it took rescuers one hour to free me from the wreckage. At the hospital, I discovered my hip was fractured, needing to be pinned, and my hand was broken. During the six months that I was recovering, hobbling around on crutches, I had tons of time to look at my life. Each

time I reviewed the accident, there were only vague
clues of what I was supposed to learn.

A few years later, I gave the details of this experience to a woman, Bernadine, who helped many
people understand their spiritual lessons. I described
the fear that preceded the accident. She asked me,
"Did you ever ask, inwardly, what message the fear
held for you when it first started? Did you ever say,
'what does this warning mean?' Did you ask if the
fearful feeling was sent to you from a spiritual guardian to get your attention and alert you to impending
danger? Did you know that accidents like yours can
sometimes be avoided—if you ask how?"

Although this sounded simple, it never occurred
to me. I thought feelings of fear were always negative, and I worked to banish them from my mind. In
one minute the light went on in my heart and mind. I
realized that it wasn't negativity invading my life,
each time I felt fear about driving. An inner helper
had tried to get my attention, and I did not recognized it.

Now, whenever any negative feelings enter my
mind, I challenge them and calmly ask, "Where did
you come from? Are you a messenger from the pure
realms of light and sound? Do you have a message
from Divine Spirit? What is it you are trying to tell
me?" Since I have learned to ask these questions, I no
longer need to battle negative feelings. Instead, I

listen for their wisdom. Sometimes the feelings that I previously considered negative are letting me know that I have been neglecting my health or my marriage. Other times they have a more subtle, spiritual message.

Take a moment to go within and ask these questions about any frightening or disturbing situation in your life. Asking these questions immediately after you complete your daily spiritual practice is the ideal time, while you are still in a heightened state of clarity. Be willing to hear the truth.

One-Minute Meditations on Wisdom and Responsibility

Use your inner ears to listen to what is said without words. Use your inner eyes to see what is alive, yet has no outer form.

◆

When you contemplate, you view an idea or thought from as many different viewpoints as possible, not holding or clinging to any one. Consider how many viewpoints you are able to embrace in one moment.

◆

Wisdom is like poetry, containing the recognizable rhythm of eternal truth. Love is like music, the voice and breath of God in expression. When they are combined to create a beautiful song, they have the power to send the heart and mind soaring to great spiritual heights.

◆

Contemplate the difference between intelligence and WISDOM. Mankind has grown considerably in intelligence, often creating chaos. Wisdom sees far into the future and recognizes that all acts of the moment affect life in the eternal sense.

◆

Take a long, deep breath. Find stillness, fix your mind on Divine Spirit, and ask, "I desire to know of wisdom and the difference between the real and unreal."

◆

Consider this: could cruelty and crime grow in a society where humans kill animals for sport and mount them as prizes? If the highly-educated have dead animal heads hanging in the same room with books, what kind of knowledge are we gaining?

◆

Turn up the volume on your self-talk for one minute. Listen to your thoughts and observe their direction. Self-talk or inner talk is a free-flowing conversation that we have with ourselves. It may be inaudible because of noise or distractions, and it is typically about beliefs we have held for a long time, or new beliefs we're in the process of accepting.

◆

If self-talk is negative, it can have a limiting effect on our lives. If it is positive, it can have the opposite effect. For one moment, just listen and learn, do not judge. The direction of the self-talk is the direction of our energy.

◆

Do you dread change? Consider this: when you cling and hold on tightly to the experiences and people you love, you also hold on to the experiences and people you dislike. Why? Because your state of being has not learned how to flow, relax, and release.

◆

Ancient Chinese wisdom says: *"Can do—DO,"* *"Can't Do—Still Learning."* This is the philosophy that banishes guilt and fear and honors creativity and compassion.

◆

Ask yourself if you've been offered genuine assistance in your life, and if you have accepted or refused it. We have greater energy and are able to sustain the upward flow for longer periods when we accept the support others are offering. When our intelligence is joined to our hearts, we are able to give and receive in a balanced way. Observe your conversations. Is there a balance of listening and talking?

◆

Silence is the gateway to Divine Spirit. Enter SILENCE as you would enter a warm, fragrant garden. If Silence feels cold, you have mistakenly entered the gateway to Loneliness. Pause, and state clearly, *"It is Silence I seek."* Allow it to find your heart. Stillness attracts silence. Once you have become adept at entering into Silence, let yourself be filled with the love that issues from the heart of God.

Spiritual Hunger
Is Satisfied

This is a story that traces the events of my own awakening and how each of us can overcome disappointments, difficulties, and tragedies.

In my early years, I relied on my ego and manipulated people and events, causing heartache. Although this was not my intention, a small bit of wisdom escaped me: your quality of life is sustained, or drained, by the energy connected to your heart and mind. When I opened to miracles of the moment, I ceased my struggle and rode the wave to my own awakening.

As a teenager, the well-meaning advice of my parents did not banish my feelings of discontent. I dreaded a future filled with spaghetti and meatballs, eaten in a crowded kitchen with a dozen people talking at once. I craved the adventure and beauty I experienced only in books.

By the time I went to college, I became obsessed with finding true love to transform my mundane life. I chased my idealized version; nothing less would do. Most of my friends were male, and they dreaded hearing about my heart's longings.

"Don't you wonder if you'll ever find true love and understand why we are here?" I'd ask.

In cold, dreary Utica, New York, they wanted only to enjoy a few beers and fantasize about getting lucky.

"Find something to do with yourself, have fun, and forget true love," my friends said. "Be thankful if you find love for a weekend," they laughed.

A direct answer from God would have satisfied me, but I had not yet met any credible person who had seen God's face or heard the Divine Voice.

When I was twenty, I met an Indian yogi and I felt excited about having an initiation. We entered a private room together, and he directed me to sit, while he stood behind me. He placed his hands over my eyes, and I began to see swirls of brilliant light. After what seemed like hours, I telepathically flashed him a thought, "I can create this kind of light show for myself—do you have anything else to teach me?" He instantly backed away and replied, "You already have an inner teacher; you don't need me." I knew I had an inner teacher, but my search was about knowing what to do with myself moment-to-moment.

My life continued in this way for a long time. New cities and new faces provided some relief from my restlessness. Tucked away in the back of my journal, I kept a newspaper clipping about "Boat People" who came to America from Asia. When interviewed and asked how it felt to be without a home, one of the children had replied, "We have a home; we just haven't found a place to put it yet." I saved this story because it echoed my own feelings. I had a great love. I just hadn't found a place to put it.

Family life was too routine. The corporate world was no place for someone lacking the aptitude for politics and small talk. Money was a means to an end, a way to be independent, and rarely held my interest. While I had lofty ideals about serving humanity, I wasn't compassionate enough to work with the sick or poor.

I longed to share the serenity of being I experienced in quiet moments, when nature spoke to me through the presence of a solitary swan floating on the lake or while gazing at a glistening, turquoise-gold sunset. Even the roar of the ocean as it crashed against the rocks carried me far beyond any experience I had had with other people.

While this was going on, the world continued as before. The names of presidents and the geography of war and famine changed. Ninety-two percent of the people on the planet did not own a car, yet Americans were still spending their lucky coins as fast as they could get their hands on them.

For a while I went to every church, ashram, and spiritual gathering I heard of. I longed to meet saints and sages who could tell me about love and give me renewed hope. After years of wild searching, disappointment crept deeper into my heart. *Greed for enlightenment is no different from greed for worldly possessions, I thought. It is a self-centered process that leads to disillusionment.* Night life in the ashrams held the familiar romantic entanglements and triangles I ran from. Daylight revealed personality conflicts and power struggles. Only the prize changed. In the Western culture, it was more money and prestige through business and marriage. In the Eastern religions, the prize that brought status was more recognition from a guru.

Everyone who was unwanted as a child and unfulfilled as an adult seemed to be flocking to a guru, seeking the elusive experience of love. I saw myself in the eyes of each lonely seeker. Maybe the mystics were playing a cosmic joke on everyone who gave up everything to gain enlightenment. Or, perhaps they were making a living in the same way as their ancestors.

Sometime around 1976, I awoke, thinking, *"I no longer want to spend time analyzing my life. It isn't necessary to dissect the petals of a rose to love its fragrance."* I wondered where that thought came from, because it possessed more confidence than my own voice. I knew that true mystics had hidden themselves from the masses, and that a softening of the heart made spiritual practices come to life. Perhaps my cynicism about enlightenment was hasty.

I darkened my room by covering the windows. Sitting quietly on the floor, I closed my eyes and asked for an experience that transcended my limitations. After what seemed like hours, I moved into another reality, as if watching an animated, color movie. There, in the middle of a council meeting, I counted thirty-two men and women. They looked human, except that their hands and feet were soft and luminous, and they seemed to glide rather than walk. They were excitedly discussing imagination, and why it was so difficult for humans to use this divine gift. *"Only a handful have learned the key to sustaining continuous imagination and riding it like a wave to their own healing. There must be a better way for us to teach them how to live with the confusion and chaos that causes them such stress. They rarely have the energy to finish their life purpose. They are aging too rapidly. They die in fear, before they have a chance to know who they really are!*

"We must let them know that great magic is brewing inside themselves. Millions of animals and people, old and young, are not feeling love from anyone. In the past we have been able to whisper to them while they slept; shall we call to them again? But, what shall we tell them? We have given them so much knowledge about the principles of attitude and attention being the key factors for this mastery, yet it continues to escape them when they need it most."

Ideas flowed for what seemed like hours. Finally, the group formed a clear thought: *The solid matter of their world interferes with the humans understanding. We must make truth clearer for them. We'll whisper to them nightly and simply say, "When you are in harmony with the time line and the blessings from the Divine Source, the confusion and suffering will dissolve. Look for one-minute healing experiences — they are everywhere! Your body will feel lighter when you encounter them; your face will look younger when you listen to them. It takes only one minute to heal."*

When I opened my eyes, a blue heron was outside my bedroom window. The love I longed for was spiraling and circling through the room and into my heart.

Weeks passed, then months and years. One afternoon as I walked alone on a quiet beach on Long Island, a handsome, mysterious man caught my attention. His piercing, blue eyes attracted me, and I noticed a blue heron in the sky. He stopped and looked directly at me and spoke. *"My name is ALOKIAM. I am here to confirm that your experience was genuine. It is a gem that could sustain you through the rest of this lifetime. Don't close it as you would a book; rather, carry it with you like a lingering fragrance. This message is your life's work. Go out into the world and let people know that miracles do not run by a clock. They may not believe you. They may be attached to their rituals and religions, to dogma and suffering. It is up to them to commit to acts of power or to continue on as before. You know the truth; tell them. Fill your mouth with rose petals and speak sweetly."*

Becoming a Magnet for Miracles

It's easy to be optimistic when we're on an even keel in life. This is why it's important to embrace and cherish moments of healing that are right under your nose. They create a continuity of awareness so you will always remember who you are—a magnificent spiritual hero—and you can cherish these moments as you allow them to guide you through times of difficulty.

As you internalize the essence of the exercises and stories you've read, you will awaken to many miraculous *One-Minute Healing Experiences*. They will become part of your consciousness and help you handle the internal stress of life with confidence.

When stress and pressure strike at us, we run the greatest risk of making poor decisions that eat away at our positive energy. Yet, it is in these times of stress that we have an opportunity to demonstrate virtues we didn't even know we possessed. I have moved through devastating tragedy, and it has enriched my life and carved a depth into my character that I might never have developed with an easier life situation.

Courage, integrity, humility, and compassion are not qualities possessed by characters on a movie screen. These heroic roles were written long ago, and we are supposed to be living them.

Do I have moments when I encounter invisible stress? Absolutely! My struggling has diminished as my own inner power has grown, and now I can release internal stress and relax at any moment. Events that I previously considered "miracles" are no longer mysterious or unknowable. New wisdom now reveals the meaning of what was forgotten and what appeared to be "miraculous" can now be easily grasped and understood. As we awaken to who we are, we are able to fill ourselves with spiritual love, wisdom, and power in each moment. When you remember how to do this, invisible stress will lose its power to drain and dominate you. You can discover how to move to the rhythm of the song that sings within your own heart.

If you know people who: have an ability to think clearly—overcome stress and anxiety rapidly—recover quickly from tragic and negative situations—have high self-esteem—are free from substance abuse—have extraordinary respect for the value and worth of others—smile and laugh often—then you have met people who have access to powerful spiritual medicine.

As you turn on your inner light and dissolve your invisible, internal stress, remember, you are never alone. You have made new friends, and we are here to "protect, border, and salute each other." Wrap yourself in a warm globe of light and protection, until you can stand on your own spiritual legs. And, for those of you who are walking, running, and dancing in the light, share your nectar with the world in your own unique way.

As your energy flows upward toward the stars, it touches and heals all of us. The search for the heart and soul of healing leads us into our innermost selves. As we clear the dread from our hearts and our bodies, we awaken and become exquisitely aware of the secrets the silent universe has been whispering to us throughout eternity. We are not mishaps, we are masterpieces. If you want to know this with certainty, begin asking yourself this: *What does the Divine Presence wish to experience through me in this moment?* The answer is yours to cherish.

A Message from the Author

The One-Minute Healing Experience is woven through the fabric of my being. As I write, teach classes, and conduct a coaching practice, this theme is evident.

Coaching is the most personal aspect of my work. Coaching is a profession synthesizing the best from psychology, business, transformation, philosophy, and spirituality. The key element to successful coaching is matching the right client with the right coach—complimentary chemistry and incredible mutual respect are essential ingredients. My clients are people who know their place in the world and are committed to making a difference. Typically they have been through some form of therapy or deep healing and live at a high level of wellness. I offer them tools and support, and I insist they honor their integrity and sacred space. After having read my own story, you will know where I have been, and the invitation to work with me is open to those who sense this mutual respect and want a relationship with a coach/mentor.

Each class and workshop I offer holds this intent: To be in an atmosphere charged with divine love, transcendent wisdom, and spiritual freedom. Immersing the Self in such an atmosphere, by a conscious act of choice, affirms and reassembles our relationship with Divine Spirit.

People often comment that they find it easier to meditate and enter the deeper realms of pure light and sound when they are in a certain environment. This is because each place—each gathering—has an atmosphere, whether we have trained ourselves to become aware of it or not.

In the words of Sri Aurobindo: "*. . . we must always go beyond, always renounce the lesser for the greater, the finite for the Infinite; we must be prepared to proceed from illumination to illumination, from experience to experience, from soul-state to soul-state.*"

AKSHAR FOUNDATION

Ellen Laura is co-founder, with Dawn Lynn, of AKSHAR Foundation.

Programs and retreats offered are for those who have an interest in embracing a deeper spirituality. Healing experiences honoring the purity, bliss, and innocence of the true self are emphasized. Through discovering how to follow inner guidance and live in harmony with Divine Essence, rather than relying solely on techniques, a spiritual awakening and illumination occurs. Seminars, workshops, personal consultations, written discourses, and books are used to facilitate this awakening.

Many people today do not have a church or a particular religious dogma with which they are in harmony. Others have left behind "gurus," and yet they still want contact with people who live a spiritual life. Workshop participants come from various religious affiliations and find themselves spiritually renewed by our association.

Religious and spiritual organizations resemble families from our viewpoint. Some provide us with a necessary nurturing and support; others are dysfunctional and corrupt. This does not mean that cynicism is the only road open to us, or that a lack of allegiance to a group is a higher path. *It is simply a reminder that any meetings involving our true spiritual allies — in any dimension — must pass this test: Are they characterized by extraordinary love and respect?*

Visit our website at *http://www.akshar.com* This is your invitation to share your "One-Minute Healing Experience" on-line. Upcoming classes, workshops, and retreats are posted on our website, or write and request a calendar of events. To be on the mailing list, e-mail to: info@akshar.com, or write:

Ellen Laura, AKSHAR Foundation
211 North Rampart, Suite 189 • Las Vegas, NV 89128

One-Minute Healing Experiences